DIFFERENCES

CIVILITY FOR ALL

NARRATED BY: SIR CLYDE RIVERS
AUTHORED BY: PROF VERNET A. JOSEPH

Printed in the United States of America

ISBN: 978-1-952963-07-0

PUBLISHED BY Live To Produce Publishing Group |Productive
Business Civility

Table of Contents

PROLOGUE

This book is meant to help you understand the race dialogue/conversations. This book is predicated as part of the movement "Civility for All." I believe that as this principle is instituted, we can solve the problems of the world. It's simple, as the golden rule is not complex. It's to love your neighbor as yourself. Now, this component is called the "Royal Law" in James 2:8. It says, "as you love your neighbor as yourself, you live under Liberty." As you continue to read down in the text, it says, "if you mistreat your neighbor, you live under a transgression." This is a component that we want to educate the world on, to love your neighbor as yourself. That's the way there will be peace and Liberty in the world.

The second component is the golden question. The golden question is this: if the shoe were on the other foot, would I be okay with the same treatment? If the answer is yes, we have a good policy. If the answer is no, then we have a bad policy. So, these are two indicators that people can use every day to help gauge the reality of their life in the arena of people treatment.

This book and this movement, Civility for All, is a key to make the world a better place. It will help you understand how to dialogue, how to communicate and how to talk with people of different races and different cultures to help make the world a better place.

CHAPTER 1

Differences

You are uniquely designed for something so great in this day and hour in the world. When we're looking at utter hatred, you have to believe like me. These are the narratives set by the world's standard today: "If you don't believe like me, you're wrong." Normally this concept occurs in left/right politics in every country. It comes down to tribalism – in elections around the world, the picture being painted is that difference is wrong. And I want to tell you, 7.8 billion people in this world are uniquely designed by God for a purpose. It is the most natural thing in the world is to be unique because you are designed uniquely. You are put in this earth for a specific unique assignment. And what we are coming down to is those institutional structures that only allow certain kinds of thinking are collapsing. Why? Because difference is the narrative.

People are created differently. They look at everything from their grid, their lens and that's difference. You are uniquely designed to see things from your perspective and what is currently taking place in the world in 2020, in the midst of COVID, social unrest, racism, all the different ills that are attacking our society. The word that people are looking at now is conformity, but conformity to an old structure and an old system is no longer the narrative that fits with a unique design. See, what happens when you start to talk uniqueness is people bring difference to the table, but difference can no longer be looked at as wrong; difference must be looked at as my view at the table gives us a new perspective to consider. As we're looking to build brand new structures, brand new institutions, you see one of the power grids of difference is when you look at some of societies' cultures that don't have every voice represented at the table when dealing with issues that involve life, the community and nations, when every voice isn't heard, the one that isn't heard can potentially be an issue.

Why? Because their voice wasn't heard in the beginning, they weren't a part of the process that establishes. So, in the beginning stages of building anything that will empower a nation, that will empower countries, that will empower cultures, that will empower institutions, you must have a representative of every culture in the conversation so that you don't lose the perspective of all. As the world becomes one global village, one global community you must reconsider what you bring to the table. When you look to any institution, there must be diversity at the table and the population of where you live needs to be reposted. And now you even must look beyond that perspective because of the virtual world; the virtual world has made the world one global village. So now every idea from different cultures, different people must be considered in the arena of how to take the world to the next level. So you are put here with an unique design, an original thumb print, an original idea and that original idea will help solve problems somewhere in the world. Your unique design does not need to be refined. It's your design and you are designed to produce something great in this world. Your difference isn't wrong. Learn how to get your voice heard at the table and let that be a part of the information base that moves institutions, the world, and knowledge forward.

I look at everything that has gone on in 2020, and the one thing that it has showed everyone is the entire world is asking for something different. I think about the pandemic, the elections, and all the other things that were going on all around the world. The truth is there was conflict and chaos over everything. Why are people asking for something different, because they are tired of the status quo. I was thinking about the information highway. Let's take that, for example, the information that people had a year ago, how much of it is relevant today? Now, watch this, I tell people we're in the revelation age. It's going to take new thoughts, and new ideas to move any industry, any institution and any individual's lives forward.

We used to live in an age where information was King, but now people are in what we would call information overload. Now, there is a hunger for revelation. People need revelation for application because you can talk about it all you want. You can read about it in a book all you want, but let me tell you something, until you get a divine download that is going to transform and change people's hearts and minds for the situation that they find themselves in no one wants to hear it. Today is a new year, but what you have to understand when it comes to differences, you've got to be prepared to pivot. You've got to be prepared to shift, and you've got to be prepared for what we call change.

Many people bark, look down or frown upon this thing that is called change, but change is inevitable. What you have to do is get in front of change. You don't want to be on the back of change. Most people live their lives in the shadow of what could be, but it is imperative that we bring leaders, young minds, global agents of change, ambassadors, and people of influence into the realm of being on the forefront. Do you want to know why you remember momentous leaders? It's because they understood differences, but they also understood being on the forefront of change. You don't remember number two; you don't remember the person who sat in the background or let everybody go first. You remember the one who broke through the barrier that you remember.

We are now in what we would call a regulatory state. It's time for us to take the revelation that we get from God as a heavenly download and put it into practical and applicable bites. Helping people to understand before there was a vehicle, before there was a carriage, before there was all that; all people had was a left foot right foot. There had to be a mind that said walking is okay, but wouldn't it be cool if we could ride, wouldn't it be cool if we could sail, wouldn't it be cool if we could fly. Every single day change is happening, and change is a result of the difference that people actually see and experience.

As the world opens back up, every institution will open with one word and open up different, nothing is going back to the way it was. This is why it's so important to have differences and the difference maker. You know what the difference maker is? I want to make this practical. Every business this past year has sat in a meeting and had a think tank or mastermind group to come up with different ideas. So difference is what is going to rule the world. I was telling people during our election, we had two schools of thinking that clashed, two schools of thinking that thought different and out of that came differences. Nothing ever stays the way it was because God is progressive. He said, he sent a Holy spirit that will lead us and guide us into all truth. Truth is moving, increasing and expanding. I just believe that this is a day where the Bible says "the earth is the Lord's and the fullness thereof." God is not taken off guard by what's going on. He has another revelation of which is differences.

Imagine yourself being at war. And when you're at war, there are two sides to the battlefield. Each side believes wholeheartedly that they are correct, that they are righteous, and they are the ones that should prevail, right? What is that? Two different schools of thought, right? Differences that people have that are now coming against one another to collide and to clash. Difference and differences are not necessarily wrong, it's just different. And when we pick that up, Hey, you think this way, and I you think that way, is there a median? Because there is more that joins us then there is that separates us. We just have to choose which side we want to be on. We get the opportunity to travel all around the globe, meet leaders of all types of classes. Why is it that we are accepted everywhere we go? We've learned when histories collide there is an avenue of approach and that's where most people miss it, because they want to come to your country, your state, your region, your island, but they want to bring their old mentality. And when you look at diplomacy, when you look at just understanding cultures, if you don't embrace differences, you're going to be left behind.

I've been in meetings for the last couple of weeks and, you know, there's times where we disagree. And I tell people, I don't have that revelation yet. That's great that you have it, but I just don't have that revelation yet. When I get it, we can talk about it, but at this current time, I don't have that understanding. Thank you for bringing that to the table. There are times when they don't have my revelation or understanding. One of the things that I've learned is this, when histories collide, it's the way forward to back off and not try to win. I'm telling you, when you try to win the argument with your way, you just shut down communication.

The way to move forward is simply say, I don't have that understanding, can you please explain to me? And let me show you what I have, and let's see the way forward. I want to help people with the process because they look for perfection and everything you deal with is process. Recognize you're going to get some of it right, but you won't have it all right! I want to change people's mind to process over perfection, because they're constantly change happening in life. We're living in processes. People are locked into the mind of perfection, but I am saying no; it's a process. God, in his wisdom, through this last year has actually shut down intellect. I wonder how many people's new year's resolution last year happened.

I love is insight and vision, because insight and vision doesn't concern itself with the circumstances that surrounds it. When we begin to look at that, the word process means that you're going through something, that means there's some systemic way that you have set to complete something. You see, when you have vision, you get to see the end of a thing from the beginning. And when you can see the end of the thing from the beginning, then you recognize there is process. Let's really dive into that for a moment. You can't have perfection, but you can always have process. When you have process and you work process, you come up now with the next word progress.

You can become progressive. You can move forward in what it is that you desire to do. Unfortunately, people are always looking for perfection. And on this side of heaven, there is no perfection. What we have to get when we begin to talk about differences, is what are differences? Differences is simply a point or a way in which people or things are not the same. Now let's make it extremely plain. The way we think, the way we do things, the way we like things, how we appreciate things, there are differences, but guess what? God made it so that we can come together. If men and women can come together, then what on earth is a difference that we cannot overcome?

This is where we start to help people understand that life is truly a process. It's something that you're going through systemically to get to progress. Evidence and results only come when you put in work and have sweat equity. Well, differences are put in place so that you can navigate the space and get a better understanding. Again difference doesn't mean that you're wrong, it simply means that it's different. What you drink in the morning, whether it be orange juice, whether it be milk, whether it be water, whether it be tea. That just depends on what part of the equator you happen to be. Does it mean you're wrong? No, if someone decides that they want to have breakfast at night, are they wrong? It's just different! We want to see things, from a civility lens; which is love, kindness, and a respect lens. And when you look through those three lenses, you begin to see differences for what they are. They are unique identifiers that help us to learn how to co-exist, that's it.

These things are so necessary to hear in this day and hour. Think about from day one when the earth had nothing, people obviously had to communicate and dialogue to progress to the state we're in now. So see, people of like differences have worked together and built great things. Now the whole key is this, many of our narratives teach us to major on the minor. And when you major on the minor, you missed the big picture. The big picture is God has 7.8 billion people with uniqueness. If you have a uniqueness, that means you are going to look at things differently. We've been taught that difference is wrong because institutions want to form us to a thinking, but the institutions can no longer maintain God. In this day and age, God is breaking out of these institutional systems that have created a thinking that want people to think a certain way.

God says, no, I'm doing something different today. And at the end of the day, we're coming from a biblical worldview.

If you don't have our viewpoint, we're not angry at you at all. It's okay for you to have a different viewpoint. Our lens is a biblical worldview. And even in our faith, if you don't agree with us, we love you. We're going to be civil with you because we understand you have the right to a different thought than I have.

I love looking from that lens because most people they don't understand, nor can they fathom how it is possible for two different thought patterns or processes to come together. We are not here to debate, hate or have issues or concerns. What we're here to do is stress a point and give you a biblical worldview. Whether you're this faith or that faith, whether you're this color or that color, whether you've been on earth for a small time or a long time, we love you. At the end of the day, we are here to make a difference. How can we 7.8 billion people on the planet learn to co-exist and cohabitate. Do you understand how sweet it would be? If country to country, state to state, island to island would have a cohesive mindset and only want to do one thing, and glorify God? Could you imagine a world where everyone brought their best and no one was competing, but they were finding ways to come alongside other people. I'm not here to compete with anyone. I know what God has called me to do. So instead of me trying to compete with you, I will come alongside you and compliment you from my lens.

People are too afraid to embrace change, embrace differences that they can't see what is ahead. God always wins! Let's look at South Africa, and apartheid. It seemed impossible but look at every situation in the world that was oppressive. So at some point differences make the difference. You can look at something for a long time, but a difference maker will make the difference. Nelson Mandela was a difference maker. Professor Vernet A. Joseph is a difference maker in Productivity. Sir Clyde Rivers a difference maker in World Civility. If this is true, then, 7.8 billion people are difference makers and God needs them to be what they're called to be. If you're oppressing, if you're suppressing, if you're depressing, you will lose because the God that liberates people will liberate every system of oppression. I heard Desmond Tutu say "there were times where it seemed impossible to change, whatever comes, but we kept asking God, and one day that change took place." God will always WIN! The God that made 7.8 billion people and loves them all; He's going to win.

Differences has been the thing that has held states, countries, islands, and regions of the world back because we're so fixated or focused on the things that separate us, that we're not allowing ourselves to see all the things that bind us at the end of the day. Do you know that all of us have three basic needs?

1. We all need a creator. I don't care who you are, whether you acknowledge it or not.

2. We all need food.

3. We all need some form of shelter.

So you need a source, you need nourishment and you need coverage. And when you see yourself in those three simplistic phases, you now start to see, there is more that brings us together then there is that separates. Difference is not something that should literally tear us apart.

It should be something that brings us together and binds us like glue. This past year has done something that I hope people can recognize, this past year gave sight to the blind. It gave hope to the hopeless. It literally gave faith to those who were in fear. I just want that to settle in for a moment, for most people, because I got my faith back on another level, because there were differences. I'll say it to you this way, and you've heard it before. It was the worst of times, but it was the best of times because there were differences. When you begin to understand how important your perspective and vision is, then everything else changes.

I've always told people, you can drop me in the middle of the jungle and I will still be productive because that is in my DNA. Differences aside, you have a choice to make fight or flight, but here's the question, why fight when you can embrace. Differences allows the world to go around. Don't run or hide from them, embrace them, understand them so that you can go forth in them. Life is going to happen to us all. If you don't believe me, just continue to live and you will see differences on a daily basis.

Everyone is important to somebody! You may not make a difference for everyone, but you'll make a difference for somebody as someone needs you to be the difference maker. In 2021, we are looking for, and we will be bringing to the stage, the difference makers so that you can hear and become a part of a stage that we created to make a difference.

CHAPTER 2

Boxed-In Thinking

————◦⟨⊗⟩◦————

We must open our eyes and look at the world we live in today. We live in a world where thinking can be acquired through any means by virtual systems and virtual instruments that allow different forms of thinking to come through. The smartphone is an instrument that allows philosophies of thinking to come through to everyone in the world that has access to this apparatus. Institutions, education, and governments have protocols, systems and structures that, if you're going to play and function within them, you have to operate according to the design of the system. Now that thinking is being challenged. Today. We have elections that are taking place in countries of the world. Every country has a right and a left side and the views of each of those sides are locked in. People can make you feel like if you don't believe like them, you're wrong.

Well, you're not wrong, different isn't wrong. Just because they have a fixed view or a fixed belief system doesn't mean you have to have that belief system. You are not wrong. Diversity, difference of thinking, is what makes the world go around. When you're looking to build something for a nation, for a group, for a business, you need to have diverse thinking at the table and not boxed in thinking. Boxed in thinking is a thought process that at some point, if you don't grow, will cause you to lose your institution. Your way of thinking becomes obsolete. When it becomes obsolete, you always have to have new, innovative thinkers to help progress your paradigms forward. Boxed in thinking only works and helps institutions grow for a season.

There will be a day where that methodology becomes obsolete. And when you try to fight for an obsolete system, that system will eventually die because progress will take place. So we, in this day and hour, need to understand that different thinking isn't wrong. And one day, what was the cutting-edge thinking narrative will become an obsolete voice. This is why boxed in thinking can kill organizations, can destroy nations, can destroy systems because it's good while it lasts, but you have to progress and know that there will be a new way of thinking that's different and different isn't wrong. Difference is what creates movement; difference is what opens people's perspective and perception to new ways of doing things. So when thinking gets boxed in, it will one day become obsolete. When it becomes obsolete, what used to produce will no longer produce. And when you fight for the old, it dies. Diversity, different thinking, looking at things from different ethnic standpoints, different cultural standpoints, different educational, and different economic levels gives you a true perspective on how to progress forward based on firsthand knowledge from individuals that think different. Different isn't wrong, difference is what takes place. And one day we will all experience difference.

CHAPTER 3

My Thoughts Matter, Your Thoughts Matter

————⊂⊗⊃————

You know, when looking at the world and the state we're in today with COVID-19 social issues, racism, multiple things around the world, the pandemic of the Coronavirus has transformed people's thinking because the operating systems of yesterday are no longer relevant for living life today. The systems of data have been changed because the structures put in place were put in place based on a narrative that didn't consider the Coronavirus. Coronavirus has shut the world down and has caused different ways of operating; different ways of getting along have been implemented to protect humanity at the other end of the coin. What takes place now is new thoughts. My thoughts matter, your thoughts matter. This is the day where the narrative of innovation will drive the way because the system that was operating under a narrative that it was comfortable with and used to seeing all the data predictions in the future is now obsolete because there's a new equation added to it.

And that equation is the world has been shut down. We must open our eyes to the 7.8 billion people that have new ideas because when you face a paradigm that hasn't existed before, and it's created a different lifestyle, a different way, you must now look for new ways of getting things done. New ways of living, new ways to operate that come from innovation. This is why differences are so important in this day and hour; figuring out how to change the world, how to open the world back up, will come through different people's perspectives. This is an hour where you would hate to have people that think in a box. If you have one-way thinkers in a day like today, you can't progress forward because the information that boxes them in is no longer the information relevant for today.

So, this is showing the importance of difference. Differences are one of the most beautiful things in the world when you know how to work with them. Differences cause us to have to think about people in a different way. Civility. When you treat people with civility, you have the ability to glean and learn from their ideas, from their experiences. And in this day, this hour, those experiences could quite simply help you establish what you need to build the future of your city, country, or organization. This is why difference is dynamic. And the ideas that are opened up in this kind of a season show the world the importance of differences. We have to open our eyes and understand that everything is not the cookie cutter way anymore. Diversity and difference are the leg and the mechanism to move things forward is getting different ideas from people. Different is the way that will help us move our nation, institutions, and organizations forward. So people need to embrace differences. The world needs to look through a different lens and my thoughts matter because my thoughts are uniquely crafted by me and for me and your thoughts matter because your thoughts are uniquely crafted for you. And together with our differences, we can build a bright future.

CHAPTER 4

Who Told You, You Were Wrong?

———— ⊂∞⊃ ————

When you look at the world today, the different extremes in institutions are telling you what's right and what's wrong. And the interesting thing is most of the media, most of the radio in different countries tell you what to think. You are told. If you think this way you are wrong, you're supposed to think this way. And when you look at politics and institutional thinking, every system has planned out how you're supposed to think. And if you don't think like that, you are classified as wrong, as narrow-minded or, even now with the elections going on in America and around the world, you are looked at as if you've lost your mind if you don't believe like me and that's both sides and that's most people. And what happens is, when you think that this is the only way you create chaos for someone; the one on the other side that doesn't believe that way is boxed into prejudgments.

They are labeled in a category and you may not understand why they believe that or what their thoughts are and that's all sides of the coin. So many times when we grow up, the institutions have already taught us and told us what to think. They didn't ask for any innovation from us. So what happens is, they have told you, "This is right. Don't do this." And what happens is those institutions that have told you that if you think differently you are wrong. But, many times they are looking for new innovation to build. So the creativity within you, that makes you different, is the same creativity that can cause their institutions to grow and expand. And what takes place when institutions tell you what to think is, at some point, that paradigm becomes obsolete. And when that paradigm becomes obsolete, many times you'll get an A+ in an assignment that is no longer relevant, because you were told what to think, and you were told any other thinking is wrong.

Well, there's a major problem with that because when things evolve and change, the way that you were told is the only way is no longer relevant. So everyone that's locked into that mindset keeps growing older with the same mindset. This is how we end up with the older generations fighting the young generations, because of thought patterns from their day that they never let go of. And then when things become obsolete, when brand new technology changes and things are moving at another level, those institutions, those patterns, are no longer relevant. So when you have an idea, always look at the epistemology of who created that thinking. And you must realize that that thinking is good for them, but it may not be good for you. So always look at the epistemology of the person that's given the rules for how to think. And many times you'll find out that their thought patterns don't match where they came from. You'll be amazed sometimes at the lack of rooting they have in what they believe.

This is why it's so important that you question, look at, find evidence that tells you that thinking is valid. And if you think different, that's okay; bring your narrative to the table, but bring it with civility, bring it with kindness and bring it with respect. You are not wrong in the thinking you have, but never be afraid to weigh your thinking against another system and check your thought pattern. If your system of thinking is good, you can make the old system obsolete by your innovative thinking. So always look at where the mentality that wants you to think a certain way, look at where that mentality came from.

CHAPTER 5

A Difference of Worldviews

———— ⬡ ————

The challenge facing us today is a difference of worldviews when you're sitting at a table, when you're in a debate, when you're discussing politics, when you're looking at sports teams, when you're looking at different countries, every individual in this world has a worldview. Some may not be able to define what their worldview is, but they have a belief system and they have a thought pattern on the way that the world should work according to their belief system. If you have eight people, you have eight different worldviews. You have different perspectives that come from different experiences and different views. Now the power of this, the power of understanding your worldview when you come to the table and there's diversity, and there's different forms of thinking, and there's different information that needs to be acquired at that table is when we're able to sit down at the table and understand different worldviews, it gives us the ability to have a rounded view of the topic of discussion. Then, people have a better chance of creating a solution, a way forward with everyone's thoughts and it's possible to move it forward with everyone feeling like they're a part of the solution.

Now, the other side of the coin is your worldview. Never, ever be embarrassed of your worldview and never be afraid to speak your worldview. You have a right as one of the 7.8 billion people in the world. You have the right to have a worldview, a different view. Many times what takes place is, there are dominant views and everyone doesn't fit into that structure. So to speak your worldview is very challenging because it comes up against other worldviews. And sometimes I call these schools of thinking; your worldview is a school of thought, thoughts that you were educated in, that you acquire through living and it's created a way that you look at the world. So everyone doesn't look at the world through the same lens. And one of the challenges that we face in differences is that people assume that other people think like them, that they reason like them and people need to look at the world the way they see it.

Those narratives are causing that, that type of thinking is creating things in the world that we're going to have to clean up. And we're going to have to deal with it, because when someone doesn't believe your way, it's still okay. What is the solution? When we don't think the same, when we have a different worldview, you can, at times when you come together with different worldviews, find a way forward. Sometimes when you come with a worldview, you may not be able to find a way forward; when you can find a way forward, make sure both people agree and you do move forward and when you can't agree , you have to agree to disagree and wait and create a different idea. Or if it's a political thing, wait till the next election and build your team of people that think like you and go vote. This is the way to deal with differences from a stability standpoint, because different doesn't mean wrong, but it also doesn't mean everyone will embrace your view. So be comfortable listening to other people's views because other people's views come from other people's experience and their experience is not right or wrong. It's just their experience. And everyone has a freewill and everyone has the ability to have their own worldview. Make sure in your worldview that you treat every human being in the world with kindness and respect.

CHAPTER 6

Generational Differences

———————⟨◇⟩———————

One of the important elements to understand about differences is we have three generations, we have an older generation, a generation in the middle, and a younger generation. Now all three of these generations grew up with a different way of thinking a different culture and a different time period. What makes this a challenge about governing is each of the three generations look at everything from a different scope, from a different perspective. And along within the perspective of the three generations, you have different individuals with unique ways of saying things and unique ways of thinking. So differences have to cross generations. If you're going to have an effective society, you have to have generational dialogue where everyone feels like they're welcome at the table. And differences that are embraced are what push the nation, the world industry, and education. It's what pushes everything forward. Now the challenge of having three generations in one is when you get the hard liners that are stuck on the idea that this is the way it's been done and it needs to go back to that.

Well, let me give you some truth. Nothing ever goes back; life will only progress forward. So it's very important when understanding differences and looking at differences from different people's eyes. The power is in looking at the difference with an objective mind and open mind and see what each generation wants to bring to the table is relevant for moving the future forward. Because we must begin to realize that young people are 100% of the future, and whether you like their ideas or their thoughts now, they will become a thought pattern of the future. So differences from cultures can be one of the greatest benefits we learn how to operate. Can you imagine having the wisdom of an older generation that can help alleviate and avoid the mistakes that they made or view other times; having a mentor or someone seasoned that has your best interests at heart and can help you avoid pitfalls that they made.

But this is why it's so important to understand differences. When you look at differences and the way to make differences work, there has to be a civility mindset. When dealing with all, we must look at every generation of justice. We must hear what they're saying and not get stuck thinking our paradigm is the only right way. When we can listen, we learn from each other. We can progress things forward because what happens every time a generation changes the paradigm of information increases. And with that increase of information and operating system change methods of doing things do not look the same. So it's very important to engage every generation and get a truth of how you're going to move it forward. Now, when talking about everyone bringing their different ideas to the table, there will not be agreement from some people. Some people will not understand.

Some people will not agree. So at that point, we have to do what's best. Get the experience, modify, and look for differences. I look for people that can enhance and bring different schools of thoughts. Different perspectives are very important at the table. They are what caused your institution to win and grow. Because if you don't grow, your school of

DIFFERENCES – CIVILITY FOR ALL

thought will not be on the forefront of the world one day. So you must understand how to keep your thoughts alive. You work with different people, you work at differences and get the input from everyone so that there's rounded information on how to move things forward. So in order for this to be progress, there must be civility. We must be kind and respect each other's opinions, each other's thoughts. How we will move the nation forward is difference. If key differences can help us see clearly what we're looking at can help us clearly hit our objectives.

I've been looking at things through this past year. I've seen and had conversations with individuals that think so differently that I'll never get. I was talking with a world leader and he told me something. He says, every generation has met three kinds of thinkers, the old generation, the middle generation, and the young generation. And he said, they all think differently. The key to government and the world is how do you merge these three into one? I was noticing when I spoke to the older generation, they couldn't see what the younger generation was seeing. I discovered you can grow up, but still live in the same paradigm. If you grew up with the same friends from the time you were young and you don't expand out into anything new you will remain the same. You can be 80 years old and think like 80 years ago and think that it is relevant because you haven't engaged change and differences.

Many people truly are living in a bubble. They're living in the bubble of their youth or their time, or their generation; the same music that they used to listen to, food that they ate, the places that they went, they're still living in that bubble. And when we begin to delve into generational differences, you're going to find how weird and how strange it is to be stuck at that step. Honestly, we're living in 2021 and they made songs about partying like its 1999.

Can you imagine not growing past your generation, not growing past your youth or your adulthood, could you imagine staying there? Could you imagine seeing a 50-year-old toddler? That is the imagery that we want you to understand as we dive into this. When we talk about generational differences, it's literally the differences that appear in the values and the beliefs and the opinions of people of different generations. In this day and age with the information highway, the worldwide web, with all the stuff going on around us, how could you possibly stay in a bubble? There are some that still are, but for the most part, most people are walking progressively. Most people are embracing change every single day. Most people are absorbing wisdom and knowledge, whether it's through books and information, college education, or revelation, people are changing every single day. We have to be careful not to negate what we would call the generational gap. It is so important for us not to sweep that under the rug, because there is a segment of our population that are still in their generational bubble.

Progressive, what a word, think about that for a moment. Have you heard the phrase those guys are progressive? Life progresses, God progresses, God moves things forward. People look at verbiage and go that's bad. God's given me more revelation to move forward every year and every day of my life. We understand that life will never go back to what it was. Tell me a time where God has gone backwards, his understanding, his information, his actual revelation grows. Look at our lives where I was last year, he progressed me. He moved me into what I'm doing today. He's taken me and as many as are led by the spirit of God.

This week I was in Vegas. I was talking to a couple of young men that I drove over to have a meeting with. One of the guys said, don't talk to me about the God of my parents. I said, wait, of your parents? He says, yeah, they were hypocrites. They would do this and that, so we don't want their God. We want God! He told me, that generation portrays an image of God that he did not want to buy. He said, I'm hypocritical too and I'm not blaming everything on them. But he said, I can't buy that God. And what he was saying was I haven't purchased that thought process from that generation.

Let's really dig in right there because most people don't understand what was just said there. I don't want the God of my father or my mother or whatever. The weird thing is, the verbiage is flipped. It's not about not wanting the God of your father or your mother or your parents or grandparents because honestly it's a new year, but he's the same God. The difference is how have you perceived or how have you received him? And when we begin to really peel the onion back, let's talk generational differences. Well, in the 1920s to the 1940s, you had traditionalists. And in 1946 to roughly about 1964, you had what we call the baby boomers. And then 1965 to 1980, you had generation X. Then people begin to say, if you were born in 1981 and after you're a millennial, but people have really now begun to understand, Hey, you don't classify everybody as a millennial.

There's also generation Z, which starts 2001 to now 2020. When we look at these five or six classifications of generations, the God of 1925 is the God of 2021. The difference is, have you perceived, or have you received that God correctly? And that's why it's imperative to have a personal relationship with God yourself, because we all know that we heard versions of the Bible through our parents and grandparents that later, when we began to study for ourselves, it sounded alike, but there were some unique differences. We began to understand it for ourselves and we began to digest it. We understood it and let it take root and flourish in us to where, when they begin to look, what manner of God is Jesus, but he's the same God. So, when we say, I don't want to buy their version, you're just talking perspective. Now what you have to do is get to the understanding of who the source is, the creator of heaven and earth. You and I, Jacob, Isaac, Abraham, your whole lineage, but he's the same God. Now what we have to ask ourselves is what were the differences that we didn't understand? Here's the real kicker, many of these generations, traditionalists, baby boomers, generation X, millennial, generation Z; they only could interpret God from where they were.

Now we have more technology, more opportunities and more education. We simply have more! So, we should understand a little bit better as opposed to looking at them and saying how wrong they were. How about look at, this was the level of their comprehension, and this is why they operated the way that they did. That's why we say we don't want to stay in a generational bubble because if you try to operate likes its 1925 in 2021, you will have a problem; there's no doubt about it. You will stand out like a sore thumb.

When you begin to talk about disciplines, skill sets, and spirituality there are so many differences. All of these different things in time. Time is the one thing that does not stand still, but we as human beings, we get to evolve in time. To expect something, to remain the exact same, although you have trends formed in time, that's the difference within itself. What do you think?

I can have a conversation with someone and tell what generation that they came up in. "Just all that technology, man, I don't need that." What about the guy that says, why don't we go back to calculators? Because life moved on... The information highway, different things are created. The fallacy, the hard thing is to think your truth is the only truth. Now, the Bible says be established in present truth. So, what takes place as many times in your time period? I mean, you had a truth. That was absolutely true, but God has progressed and moved into new truth. That's why he says be established in present truth. So that means truth is progressing, moving forward.

I said, look, guys, you are not going to change institutions that God wants to bring into existence. Now no man can stop that. God gets what he wants done, how he wants done, when he wants done. And he may do it without you. So, when you think about generational thinking, I am to mentor people. I'm not fighting for the stage. I am no longer trying to be the rock star where everybody knows my name. Where I see we have not done things as they should be is many people holding the stage too long. They don't know how to start to promote other people. I am so joyful every day when I get to empower other people. I get calls every day and the spirit of God told me, he says, empower everyone that calls. Do you know the things that I'm getting to impact around the world because my job is to empower, not to compete? My job is to say, this is what I know in that. Well, I'm sorry. I don't know that, but this is how I can help you right now. And that dialogue means I have to hear differences. Sometimes kids are swearing, cussing, but it's their pursuit of God. And God's with them in it and you're going, wow, that sounds horrible. No, they're coming with their reality of God. And God will help them with areas that I may think they need to change right now. God says, he's cussing right now, he swears, he's done this, but I'm trying to get my love to his heart. So, keep talking to him and don't be trying to change him. Just let my love get in. And my love can work in his heart, his language, and whatever God wants to change. So what happens is that I look at the world differently and if Christ is in, he'll do the work. We didn't walk this thing perfectly. We didn't say everything right. We didn't have every step right.

Have you ever noticed, how most people who have issues are really having issues from areas that they struggle in? Have you ever paid attention when it comes to relationships, how the person who is extremely jealous is the cheater? Have you ever sat there and really just watched the world to say, why are we having this issue? Because there's something deep down on the inside that is telling me, this is your problem. But instead of you taking the mirror and looking in the mirror and seeing what you need to work on, you projected on everyone else. And when we talk generational differences, that's exactly what happens. They don't talk like we do. They don't think like we do. Well, guess what? We weren't meant to be robots.

That's why every fingerprint, every retina is different. So, we have to learn how to embrace generational differences. When you think about a generation, what is a generation? It's a group of individuals with particular age range who may have similar ideas, attitudes, values, etc. But you have to understand there are varied thought patterns, processes, ideologies within a generation. What happens when you begin to talk about generational differences in the workplace or in the workforce? What happens when you start to talk about generational differences when it comes to politics or when it comes to religion or when it comes to relationships? We still have to get this thing right. We still have to work together. We still have to ask ourselves, how do we do better? Let's peel that onion back really quick.

Let me give like three or four generational differences. When it comes to diversity in your workplace. How do you recruit? We all have generational differences in the workplace. You got to strategize your recruiting strategies. You have to avoid making what they would call an age-based assumption or stereotype on someone. And then you got to take it a step further and listen to your employees and find out what they really want instead of trying to impress upon them what you think they want. That's just the workplace, my friends. What happens when you take it to another section or another industry or another level? That's why these conversations are so important because differences are important, but so are generational differences.

I was on a show last month with a young lady that created a program called every business needs youth. She said, we can walk in and in a couple minutes tell you where you're outdated. We can walk in and tell you how you're going to miss our generation. And every business wants to be generational, but many lose it when they stay stuck in a paradigm. She said, when I walk in, I can tell you where your technology's off, how you're missing us and we are your future customers. Tell me someone that bought a generation backwards, generations always move forward. Let me give you an example. When the cell phone first came out, I said, I don't need one of those, but six months later, I had one. When different technologies came up that I didn't think I needed, life progressed to the point to where everybody needed a cell phone. The old home phone unit is obsolete. So, we'll have said, I don't need that. How many things have you said you don't need that you have today?

Which is one of the reasons, when it comes to differences, you should never say never. Never say, oh, I'll never want that. You don't know what the future holds, that's why it's so important to make sure you don't use those absolutes because just like that, your life can change. Your circumstance can change. Your need may change. Your skillset may change. And you've got to be in a place generationally where you're willing to embrace the wisdom that comes from other generations, not just backwards or forward, but all around and everything in between. There is something to be learned by everyone everywhere every day. And if you think that you have arrived, when it comes to knowledge, I sadly want to inform you that you are incorrect because we are learners. And we are learning every single day, whether it's what's right, what's wrong or what's indifferent. How to better do something, how to become a better version of ourselves. So generational differences, differences as a whole, we want to let you know that they are here to stay in the workplace, in the marketplace, in relationships, in your finance, everywhere you turn, you better believe that there's going to be a difference. And there's going to be a generational difference.

This conversation right here is one that everyone needs to understand. No one's wrong for having a thought from their day. You must understand when the vehicle changes, your thought may have to change. When the method of transportation of your knowledge becomes obsolete you will not be able to influence and people will not listen. I love what a friend of mine said. He said, the older you get the less people listen. And I thought about that. I said, if you've mentored people the right way, that shouldn't be the case. The more you get older, the more people want to hear your wisdom and this is what I'm saying. If people aren't listening to you, do a checkup from the neck up and make sure that you are not pulling people backwards to what was because generational differences are real. The younger generation are 100% of our future. So, their voice matters in the equation of their life. It's time we have a generational discussions and we learn on both sides. We're not projecting our fear of what we did wrong on to them and it's a dialogue and not a monologue.

When we talked about differences and generational differences, imagine it from a hospitality mindset because the hospitality industry is what takes care of us as a people. So, when you begin to take this train of thought into that arena, there are three major things that they say:

1. You want to make sure that you look at the people who are young in age, but may be old at heart, young age, but maybe old at heart.

2. You've got to learn how to achieve a wider brand scope by narrowing your focus. Because at the end of the day, what you want to be able to provide is safety and security. No matter what industry you're in, you're going to have to provide safety and security. And you do that by achieving a wider brand scope, but a narrower focus. I hope this is making sense.

3. At the end of the day, you want to avoid alienating whole generations.

When you see it from that perspective, life begins to change. And you begin to say, not only do I embrace differences, I want to understand generational differences. Because at the end of the day, we all just need to learn how to get along.

We've come a long way with our differences with our battles and wars. We've come a long way in the world, but we still have a long way to go. And older generations open your perception to hear the actual young generation, and also young generations open your eyes and ears to hear because our histories are colliding so we can progress life forward. It's just different schools of thinking. And when you bring us all together and we can hear each other out without being offended, we find strategies to help you not make the mistakes we made and also to help us progress life forward for all. We need you; you need us. We're still here in the earth because God needs us to work together.

CHAPTER 7

Solutions To Differences

———⟨◦⟩———

The major tool that we must discover for solutions to differences is we each must create a listening ear, an ear to hear and a path to put new information is very important to understand that you don't have all knowledge of everything. So one of the important things when dealing with differences is you must create a different lane in your thinking where you put new information as you research and look at it. And even in the midst of dialogue and the midst of confrontational dialogue, you have to have a lens to put information and not get offended. And you have to hear what people are saying because sometimes differences are not always embraced. So people may not present their difference in a format or style that suits you. But what must happen is the information they're bringing is relevant to bring change to the table, and, if it's relevant, you must create a different lane in your thinking so you can gather the information and process it while looking at the big picture.

One of the great objectives is what is the big picture? When the big picture is something that affects both people, all parts of the table, the dialogue is very, very important when you know what the objective of difference is. When you don't have an objective that everyone agrees on, this can be very challenging, and you will have a stalemate. You must begin to understand that difference is what drives narratives, difference is what moves the world forward at different levels. Your solutions won't be perfect, they'll be a part of the process. So never be afraid to venture into different ideas when you're looking at solving problems, because with differences, you can always course correct. When it's not right, don't be paralyzed that it has to be done a certain way. You must open your mind because there are three generations in one.

And when we are not objective listeners, we begin to push our agendas and it creates conflict. Conflict is not always a bad thing. When you know how to dialogue through it, solutions will come from ideas and from people. So we must never forget that the way that we're going to solve every problem is by dialoguing with people and someone, one of the 7.8 billion people, will have an idea in the world that helps move things. And yes, thanks brother. This is what we must look at in this day and hour to progress the world forward, because difference right now is looked at as a real bad thing that if you don't believe like me, you are wrong, but that doesn't move the world forward. What moves the world forward is when there's a clash of ideas, a clash of ideologies. And I say a clash, not a war, not a riot.

And now we have the ability to sit and hear people's experience, where they got the knowledge from. And is it relevant for moving it forward today? So this is a day where there has to be a different way of listening because with the technology everyone has access to now to bring their ideas to the world. In the past, that wasn't always the pitch because information was limited. Information is no longer limited, information can be applied everywhere and everyone can put their information into social media, into the world's information bank of knowledge. So now all knowledge matters and we must be open to all knowledge, but it doesn't mean all knowledge is relevant for moving the narrative forward. So we must understand this is a day of difference. We must embrace difference with a brand-new lens within our mind within our hearts.

CHAPTER 8

Modern Day Differences

———⟨∞⟩———

This topic is going to open the eyes of a lot of people to a lot of great things that are coming in the near future. Yes, it sounds strange to be speaking futuristically, call it a prophecy or whatever it is, but modern-day differences are here to stay. So, get ready, get your heart and mind prepared to receive it today.

Let' talk to on the topic of modern-day difference-makers. Now of course there are difference makers in every decade and throughout history. Today I want to highlight the modern-day difference makers that are alive right here right now. You know, often times we find ourselves looking back into history and there's nothing wrong with that. You look back to be catapulted forward, but now in this season and for this generation, I feel it is so important for us to teach people how to appreciate those while they are alive. So, as we dive into modern day difference-makers, I want you think from that perspective and ask yourself do you know any modern-day difference-makers?

There are people in the world who will never ever tell you you're good enough to do anything. So, what I tell people to focus on is the gift and the passion on the inside. You don't need anyone to fuel you because you are enough. Never look for a kiss from the outside, go and do the needful thing and express it with your life.

I think about all the people from our World Civility platform who have started world movements, but the funny thing is, it isn't a movement; it's our lifestyle. It's a lifestyle of people that have chosen to be modern day difference makers. As such, we see life from a biblical world view. If God created everyone and God is a God of love, who does he hate?

You may not agree with everything an individual does, but he/she doesn't, not love them. Look at the oppressive institutions around the world that are holding the people that God created back because of monetary gain. That is something in the country system that holds people down. Do you think the creator of the world is okay when his people are oppressed, suppressed and depressed? Do you really think the creator of the world is okay with that?

I don't think when we actually look at our everyday life that we recognize that God is in every area, and in every instance of it. It is so amazing to me, how people actually watch things, let's put on this lens for just a moment. You are talking to someone else and you're telling them, what you expect of them. And you expect to see action, evidence and results. But for some reason, when it comes to you, putting the mirror on yourself, you more or less, govern yourself according to your intentions, but you want others to operate according to action. And that is where we begin to talk about difference makers. When we begin to talk about modern day difference makers, it is imperative for us to use the same lens that we desire of others on ourselves.

Now we know in the good book, it tells us to do unto others as we would have them do unto us. So, what is different when you're talking about a difference maker? Do you want to be a difference maker in your home? Do you want to be a difference maker in your community? Do you want to be a difference maker in terms of an influencer in a region or around the globe? Either way, when you talk about being a difference maker, there's a mindset that kind of goes along with it. And I dare to say this right now, but there was a book that we wrote that talks about *"The Making of A World Changer."* The making of a world changer brings about specific things that people can do and practice to become, difference makers.

Now, the difference that you will make may not be the same difference that I will make, but we sure will make a difference in our own, right. We're not competing. We're not here to tear one person down so you can get built up or vice versa. When we talk about our modern-day difference makers, I think we have hundreds of difference makers that are making big things happen. We all have come out of 2020, but do you know how many platforms were created because of difference makers?

You see difference makers are people that aren't afraid to interrupt or disrupt the status quo. Old systems are in existence and it's not benefiting people and it's causing things that aren't good. You see, the old system focuses on it may benefit you, but not others. And I always tell people, difference makers, ask the golden question. If the shoe were on the other foot, would I be okay with the same treatment? And so many people say, well, I'm living good. It's not ok just for you to be living good, but your brother or sister is living bad and are not free; then you're not free. Difference makers interrupt systems that may benefit one, but not the other. They look to bring equity of opportunity.

Difference makers don't let people jade the narrative. Everyone doesn't have to be equal or have equal stuff, what they need is equity of opportunity because 7.8 billion people all have a different gifts. Now, when you've lived in benefit and others haven't, it's hard to give up benefit; but don't worry about it. I love what Desmond Tutu said, he says, "God always wins." Look at South Africa with apartheid, look at the various countries in the world where people have been mistreated, a just God adjusts. God always finds difference makers to interrupt paradigms. What we're doing in this day and hour, and it's around the whole world is making a difference. We have traveled the world and seen that you can't just look at the oppression, poverty, sickness, and wretchedness that goes on in the nations of the world without having a heart to make a difference. God's not happy with that. God is raising up difference makers that are empowering other people, because you have no idea of what God's designed that person to become. One day they can be lifted to be over you.

We talk about lifting others, I am so engulfed in that, my livelihood, my lifestyle, my mentality, it's what I do each and every day. I am wrapped up, tied up and tangled in just that, it's about helping other people. And it's not about greed. It's not about myself. It's not about, put me in front of a camera or, lifting up my name. It's building platforms that other people can shine on. That is what we call selflessness, right? Not selfishness, but selflessness. And when I think about a difference maker, a difference maker is an interrupter, but also is a disruptive force that causes anything that is of ill will or ill gained to disperse. Then when we see ourselves as difference makers, modern day difference makers, we then shine a light and open up a pathway, a door, a window, a chasm for people behind us to come through.

So, as we break these barriers and tear down these walls, as difference makers, people's lives, and generations will be changed because of what we do today. As I think of that, a quote that comes to mind is the action, the preparation and the execution of today, fortifies our tomorrow. So, what are we doing? Who are some modern-day difference makers in your life, in your community, in your industry, and your region? I firmly believe that we can do more together than we can do apart.

As difference makers, your starts are ugly. How you start to be a difference maker is not pretty. Sometimes, it may be something that happened to you and you don't want to see that injustice ever again. It may be something that happened to a family member, something that inspired you to say, I'm going to make a difference. Change isn't change until it's changed. Difference makers bring a change, but it's not changed until it's changed. So, difference makers are people that create a culture for what they want to change. You have to build a culture. I Change Nations for example, is the world's largest culture of honor organization.

We saw a need for honor, so we created it. We said, wait, why is it that when I traveled the nations, all of these good people doing good, but no one, was honoring them. So, we started a business called I Change Nations. It's the world's largest culture of honor. We have been around the world, working with modern day difference makers, Christiana Kozachuk, *Every Girl Wins* as she has taken a thought and idea. And now that thing is moving in 15 nations, Dr. Robin and Lococo of *Challenge Champions and Heroes* she had a, a passion for special needs community and their care givers. The differently able need to be treated with honor and respect and its actually taken off in the countries of the world. Now, what am I saying this for? Because modern day difference makers are changing the world. Dr. Vernet A. Joseph with your Productive Business Civility. You have been acknowledging people globally that are making a difference in the Caribbean, Jamaica, Saint Martin, Anguilla, and countless areas in the world to name a few.

One of the things that really blesses me is when we begin to think about the difference makers in our lives, it may start off messy. When you start, it is not pristine or clear cut. It is not just going to fall into your lap, the way that you expected, but modern-day difference makers are those who are sold out to their belief, whatever that is, however it's going to help other people they're sold out to it. Dr. Will Moreland, who actually created "Healthy Competition," did you hear that healthy competition? You know, I think of people like Ife Badejo, who is making a difference with "Islandpreneurs" in the Caribbean and are changing people's lives around the globe. I think of Marquez Hughley, with "Crown Life" and how he's leading Christian and Business Leaders from different walks of life together to understand "21 Days of Crown Life" and Crown Life Living. Can you think of anyone in your community, in your region, in your soul that is making a difference? We are looking for modern day difference makers. This is the year, the year of the difference-maker. We want them to know that we appreciate their contribution to the earth. Listen, I don't care who you are out there right now, despite what you may be going through. Despite what yesterday may have held. What I need you to know is to stand flat-footed and firm in who God has made you to be. There's something inside of you that is going to revolutionize the world, but don't keep it hidden.

Get involved, get started right here right now. Listen, I'm reminded of another book that we put together. "I Have A Solution," it doesn't matter if you're talking about race relations or injustice, it doesn't matter if you are a speaker, it doesn't matter if you're an author, whatever it is that God has called you to do my friends, I don't want you to hold back. A great difference maker that I'm thinking about right now is TC Cooper with her "Characterpreneur" and "Faith Focus Flow" programs, and how she brings about the community to understand the dynamics of who you are. How you can lead effectively through making a difference. This is the year of the difference makers!

We have, Dr. Karen Moore with "Colorism." She's actually showing people that, the color of your skin does not define you. It does not define you as good or bad. She has a movement that's impacting the world. Dr. Julian Businge with "Royal Civility," teaching we are modern day Royals creating a new mindset in people. Anana Phifer-Derilhomme with "Blessed Girl." So, we have all these people, Professor Patrick Businge with Greatness University. What's happening is all these people, in the midst of the last couple of years have been inspired to move out of the boat.

Dr. Ruben West with "Bialogue," moving to help create a new communication paradigm. Dr. Tracey Ward with actually the "Reset Reality." So all of these people have stepped up to be difference makers. When you make the difference, Professor Vernet, the person that made a difference in your life has no idea what you're doing today and how many people you've impacted. The one that impacted my life has no idea what I'm doing today. Men never devalue the one that's to be empowered by the son of God, because you have no idea what that one will do later in life. What about the one that empowered Nelson Mandela? What about the one that had empowered Mahatma Gandhi? What about the one that inspired Dr. Martin Luther King Jr? What about the one that inspires the next difference makers? The value is making a difference for others lives.

If we can make a difference for the one that is what matters. So many people in this day and age, they're caught up in the internet sensation going viral and all of that stuff. Listen, if you can do it for the one, the one it's enough. You never know the seed that you are planting in someone's life and what, and who they were called or created to be. Many times we get to a place where we amass, what we would call or think is success, but true success of a world leader, true success of a difference maker is the empowerment of the people who they have impacted and how those people will go forth. I'm a reminded of many different pastors who they had predecessors that were giants, but God told them to pass the baton. The applause of men is the royal drug of the enemy. You don't understand how important it is to pass the baton at the right time.

When you think of these leaders, these speakers, these authors, these difference makers, these influencers, it's not just about them. It's about how many other people they can deposit seeds into. Because when you begin to have the right perspective/lens you start looking at the world and you say, I see men as trees. Oh, life begins to change because men and women are seeds grow up to be trees that, provide nurture for others. And this also it gives back to the ecosystem. So when we talk about being a difference maker, this is not a game or a fad. This is not something that you're just going to see, come up, leave you the next day. This is something that is a lifestyle. When you talk about, I Change Nations, the largest culture of honor, millions of things will be birthed because there was one seed planted who decided to take that and run with it. When you talk about becoming a disruptor and interrupter, because there's a void, lives begin to change, and we have not even seen the tip of the spear as to what is going to be accomplished.

As a leader, when you don't pass the baton, you can leave a mark in your generation, but a scar in the next one. When you don't turn the power over, you begin to create systems where people are damaged in their thinking, because it becomes more about you than it does about moving them forward. So I tell people, I want to leave a mark and I want to leave fruit that remains in every generation. Get your actual ego filled by God so that you can bless others. I've created a platform by the grace of God, and now it's time to put people on.

They're coming from all over the world to walk on this stage. They're coming from all over and I'm not making it difficult to be on the stage. When I interview and talk to people that get on the stage, I will know whether they paid the price or not by our conversation. If I didn't have certain things happen in my life, I wouldn't see that the one I need to depend on is God. He was the only one that could pull me out. I wouldn't have the faith I have today. Sometimes we try to pray away, move everything away, but it's what I went through that's made me a difference maker. So people, we can't pray the trial off your back. We can pray grace to walk through, cause that's going to cause you to make a difference. That pain you're in right now will cause you to make a difference. That thing that you don't like, that bothers you every time that's the thing that's going to make a change in the world.

I don't want to be a difference maker today only. I don't want to be a difference maker where I'm acting like Al Bundy and only talking about my high school hay days. I want to be a difference maker all day, every day. I want to impact someone's life all day, every day. And when we talk about modern day difference makers, that's exactly what we're doing now. We put a platform together that is empowering millions of people all around the globe. We're here to show you that it's possible. And if it's possible, then why not accomplish it? Why not do it get away from that adage of fake it until you make it, do what you've been called to do, what you're born to do; and shine bright so that generations can see that it's possible.

It's your time. Not a time to debate, not a time to hate, not a time to complain, not a time to have issues with this person or that person empower everyone that you come in contact with. And we talk about ego. Your ego needs to be filled with his goal. You want to be empowering God's opportunities with each and every person that you come in contact with when they come in contact with you, they've got to see a God-sized opportunity. That's what ego you need to be walking with today.

This was so important to understand difference makers. Don't do it for the accolades, do it for the obedience to God. 1% of the time you're grinding the other 99 you're behind the scenes working to the wee hours in the morning to make something happen. You're traveling in your car and on airplanes. You're going to shine for five to ten minutes on the stage, but 95% of the work that empowers others is not done behind the scenes.

It's all about civility in every single facet of life. Remember this is the year of the difference maker. The question is what type of difference will you make? Blessings, peace and civility.

CHAPTER 9

Civility For All

———————⬳———————

Civility for all what does it mean? How do we do it? How do we exercise it every single day? Now, once you understand what it means, now you can carry the torch and you can pass the torch and baton at the same time.

Civility for all is about kindness and respect for every human being in the world. That's coming from a biblical worldview because that's my life lens. I believe God created 7.8 billion people. And I believe those people, every individual is called to do something, to help 7.8 billion people. So basically, God has created people to solve people problems. And many times, in the world, we miss that component. We see them as our enemy because of a religious spirit or, and I'm not talking about a church, I'm talking about an urban religious spirit. That is a spirit of man's tradition that makes the word of God of no effect. What happens is we begin to look at 7.8 billion people that God created to solve each other's problems. At times people have been allowed to be de-humanized, murdered, and killed. And I say, we just lost contributions. What were they called to bring to the world? And until we start to value the currency of God, the gifts in people, our world, we'll go through a lot of change.

What I want people to understand when we begin to talk about civility for all, it's exactly what it sounds like. It's not civility for one group of people. It's not for a one status of people. It's not civility for the rich or just the poor or those in between; it's civility for all. When we look at the golden rule and we think about it, what are they really saying? Could you imagine a world where everyone is civil? Could you imagine a world where everyone plays their part? Could you imagine a world when differences are made on an hourly, minute and secondly basis? Because that's the world that we imagined when we created civility for all, when you establish a radio show called Civility 360, it helps you to understand the magnitude of what God is actually trying to do in, with, and through us.

Make sure that you don't miss this, many people are always asking, how is it that you can give away all this information? We are planting seeds that we know will bring a harvest. So, when we plant the seed of civility for all, we plant the seed of having the solution. We plant the seed of helping people to become difference makers, agents of change and world changers. These are seeds that we're expecting a harvest from, so much so, that we've built stages and platforms to ensure that those seeds are not only available to be nurtured, but that they would grow up and become, vineyards to their communities and their surrounding areas. So, when you hear the statement, civility for all, remember this civility is like the air that you breathe without it you cease to exist. I hope that you all are picking up what we are putting down. As we talk on a topic that is relevant and will be relevant for ages to come. There are very few things that are timeless and civility for all is a timeless factor without a shadow of a doubt.

Look around the world where there's been people oppressed and dehumanized what eventually happens is the people rise up. All these things can be avoided, if we do one thing, treat every individual in the world with kindness and respect. I didn't say we had to agree with the lifestyle. I didn't say we had to agree with what they're doing, but if we can treat people with kindness and respect things would be different. What people don't understand is the principle of sowing and reaping a yin and yang. When you sow good, you're going to reap good back. When you sow kindness, you're going to reap kindness back. Now, let me give you a quick example. Have you ever got angry at someone that wasn't angry at you and when you were angry, when you got angry with them, what did they come back with? Anger to you? So what happens when we can look at people with kindness and respect, we have a chance to move forward, to move the world forward at a better and different pace.

As we look at civility for all, what does it actually mean? It's walking in kindness and respect. It's putting kindness and respect in its rightful place. It's helping people to see and understand that we are all important, that we are all valid, that we are all worthy because at 7.8 billion people, do you think God made a mistake out of one? Of course not. He knew the exact number of hairs on the head of every one of them. At the end of the day, what God is actually saying to us is if my people who have my actual name would do the thing that they need to do, pray, which is communication with God, a dialogue with God, then I will heal the land. I see a day where civility for all is not only talked about, but it is lived out in the realms of time that it is passed down from generation to generation so that people will not only see it, not only hear about it, but that they will live it.

Textbook knowledge, street-smarts, and all of that is fine, but how are you going to execute over a long period of time? We're not here to start a fad. We're not here to do the status quo. We're here to be interrupters and disruptors so that we can change the trajectory of the lives of the people that we deal with each and every day to include ourselves. The great thing about civility for all is no one is excluded. Everyone is included; not excluded. So, whether you're sitting on the other side of the world right now in China, we love you, appreciate you, and we want to empower you the best that we can. If you're sitting in the Caribbean right now, whether you're in Haiti or St. Martin or Anguilla or any of the Western/Eastern Antilles, we want you to know that you are important to us.

As we share this principle, I dare you to take this principle and work it out. I dare you to work it out in your organization. I dare you to work it out in your life so that you can see the results. When we think from a lens of civility for all, there is freedom that you cannot possibly understand. As we continue on the year of the difference maker, we are calling on you. We're looking for you. And you may say, well, I only make a difference in this part of the world. Any difference that is made anywhere is definitely a conduit to civility for all. If it is causing people to move forward, and it is a positive movement that points people back to God, we want to hear about it.

I was speaking with law enforcement a couple months ago, and was trying to decide how do we bring this down to every community? How do we make this work in every city? You have people that are different, as difference is all around you, differences in your household, your neighborhood, and everywhere you go. There's someone that thinks and believes different than you. If I live in a community that has differences, how do I make civility for all work? Simple principle, live the golden rule with everyone in the public square, treat others with civility, kindness, and respect in the marketplace.

As I go home, I can live my life Sunday morning. When I go to my actual faith, I can do that. But in the public square, we need an agreement to treat others the way we want to be treated in the public square. So, that becomes an actual sacred place where everyone can be treated with kindness and respect, treat others the way you want to be treated in the public square.

The moment that you begin to practice kindness and respect, you can't help, but it to overtake you. Now, let me show you the thing that wraps everything all into one, the way that you're able to walk in kindness and walk in respect and actually execute those things is tied up in one word. And that one word goes before. And it goes after kindness and respect. When we think of the philosophy of civility for all. What I want you to understand is that kindness and respect can only be given when there's a true heart. Ready with love, kindness, respect, and love. Repeat love, kindness, respect, and love. If you operate with this mentality in mind, it doesn't matter if you were in the marketplace, in the world space, in your basement, or in the white house.

It doesn't matter because it will be love, kindness, respect, love, repeat, love, kindness, love. And when we begin to operate from this lens, my friends, the world will begin to change. Now, some of you may say, well, I haven't seen it happen. Listen, that may be your testimony, but that's not ours. We have seen the seed of civility for all shoot across the world and have been utilizing this principle. The question is, are you ready to utilize this principle? Because it's a game changer.

One of the important things about this is we're building a culture, a mindset that thinks kindness and respect. First, we are interrupted because we really understand that person next to me could be a solution for me. Now I'm looking at him/her differently. What if that guy is a doctor that will heal your daughter from a sickness that she has? Would you look at that person differently? What if God put a gift in them to rid the world of HIV AIDS and you had it. You have to broaden your perspective, the people you're looking at, and you hate, you don't know what the creator designed them for. We're talking the creator of the world.

If you don't agree with this, that's okay. I promise you we're not going to bother you. You're not going to bother us because you're not going to change what we believe, and we aren't going to change what you believe. I'll be kind and respectful to people that disagree, because I don't have the understanding they have. They don't have the understanding I have. I'm not looking to fight people over this. I can tell you what's taking place in my life and what we're building and where it's moving. When I began to look at people, differently, it changed my world.

A quick story, about a life changing moment. The razor phone had just come out, and I was happy cause I had service all over the world. I mean, I could call anywhere, and someone would answer the phone. I had just traveled out of the country and my flight landed earlier then schedule that morning, but I had my phone ready to go. And I was talking to people at the airport because a friend of mine was supposed to be picking me up. I had the phone number to call him, but I didn't know how to dial the phone number in this particular country. I walked up to several people and they didn't understand my accent. So, I had the power to call but couldn't. I walked around for three hours and nobody could understand my accent. No one could help me call.

No one in the country knew what the country code was to call in. So guess what happened? I finally found a gentlemen that understood me after three and a half hours. And I learned a great lesson. I may have all the power to call the whole world, but if I can't communicate with people and they can't communicate with me, I'll get nowhere. So that showed me the value of people. That small story, about having all the power really sticks with me. I was coming from the most profitable country in the world, with all the knowledge, and couldn't call a mile away. Simply because I didn't have the correct access but thank God I was kind enough, and someone knew and was willing to help me. That's just a story. So remember you can have all the power to call anywhere and do it all, but you will need people one day to help you connect where you got to go.

As we talk civility for all, keep in mind that it has nothing to do with your pedigree, your bank account or what side of the tracks you may have grown on. Civility for all is something that supersedes all of that. You can have all the right equipment, right motives and the right intent, but without access; you cannot accomplish the mission. A key point to civility for all, is the access that it gives to being a difference maker. Someone came along in that country and was able to say, I can make a difference for you. And all those people that you came in contact with, they couldn't make the difference, but there was someone that could through kindness and respect; and it was wrapped in love. Someone else came along that didn't even know you from Adam and said, let me reciprocate the love, kindness, and respect that I see in you.

And because of that access you were now able to go where you needed to go. What we are talking about when it comes to civility for all is the access to every door on earth. So now is the time for us to stand up and set up a standard that civility for all is not just a practice, but it is a lifestyle.

One of the things that we want to establish is a new way of thinking. When you begin to look at people, as I have no idea how valuable that person is, we will look at every individual in the world differently. Some people have been changed like you could never believe. God never gives up on anyone and God hasn't created any spare parts. God has 7.8 billion MVPs, and you are one of the most valuable persons in his sight. You don't solve all the problems by yourself. Somebody helps solve your problems as well. If you don't think 7.8 billion people are valuable, tell me that the last time that you had a major problem, and it wasn't a somebody that helped you solve it. Everybody is a somebody! And that's why we are promoting civility for all.

What I hope you understand and know is that life is all about civility. There is no life without civility. Civility truly is the engine that drives our world. It's the air that we actually breathe. If you begin to make small improvements daily, you will find that it is the key to growing immensely in a lifetime. We want to seek out, search out the difference makers in this world. Life is meant to be lived, not meant to be existing in. We don't want to merely exist. We want to live our lives to the fullest and living connotes to living in victory every day and life equates to living in full expectation. So the question is, are you a difference maker? If not, are you ready to make a difference?

CHAPTER 10

The Difference Maker Award

———⟨∞⟩———

The difference maker. These are specific individuals with a vision to help empower the world through kindness and respect, which is our civility narrative. These individuals are working in different areas of life with a different perspective. They understand that if we don't help everyone get to the place they're supposed to be in life, we all lose. These individuals are pacesetters, history makers, world changers, and difference makers. That is what we're looking for and what we will bring to you in 2021. Differences are the key to difference makers. Difference makers look at things differently, as they change the world; and this is why differences is the way of life. Stay tune as we highlight and honor well deserving individuals in 2021 with The Difference Maker Award.

Proactive Dialogue Starters:

Knowing you are at odds when you start, but the outcome is greater than the current reality...

I will choose to bring solutions with kindness...

I want to do better...

You want to do better...

Can we dialogue so we can do better...

We can all do better together...

Listening allows us to go through the process to do better...

Our world deserves us doing better...

We must be proactive in change...

Change will change us all...

The
STATE OF CIVILITY SUMMIT
SATURDAY, MAY 16TH
AT 2:00 PM PST | 5:00 PM EST

FAMILY CIVILITY
DR. REBECCA HARPER
(JAMAICA)

FEMALE CIVILITY
PROF. ONA MILLER
(TX)

BUSINESS CIVILITY
PROF. VERNET A. JOSEPH
(AZ)

YOUTH CIVILITY
DR. JUMA NASHON
(AFRICA)

EDUCATIONAL CIVILITY
DR. MICHAL PITZL'S
(OR)

GLOBAL CIVILITY
SIR CLYDE RIVERS
(CA)

ENTREPRENEURIAL CIVILITY
DR. RAYMOND HARLALL
(CANADA)

@CIVILITY360

JOIN US LIVE ON OUR CIVILITY360 FACEBOOK PAGE

The State of Civility Summit is developing Civility Solutions for our world through Civility In Action! Created to promote the pillars of civility through kindness, respect, love & action. Join Global World Civility Leader, Sir Clyde Rivers and Productive Business Civility Prof. Vernet Alin Joseph as we host civility in action. Topics of discussion: Family Civility, Female Civility, Business Civility, Youth Civility, Educational Civility, Global Civility and Entrepreneurial Civility.

STATE OF CIVILITY YOUTH SUMMIT
DIALOGUE ABOUT THE FUTURE & VOICE OF GLOBAL YOUTH

SATURDAY, MAY 30TH
AT 2:00 PM PST| 5:00 PM EST

BUSINESS CIVILITY
PROF. VERNET A. JOSEPH
(AZ)

GLOBAL CIVILITY
SIR CLYDE RIVERS
(CA)

DR. JUMA NASHON
(AFRICA)

ELIZABETH CURELY
(CANADA)

MATEUS MUTOLA
(MOZAMBIQUE)

ANANA PHIFER – DERILHOMME
(NEW JERSEY)

IRA ROACH III
(DELAWARE)

PSALM EBUBE
(LEGOS NIGERIA)

JOIN US LIVE ON OUR
CIVILITY360 FACEBOOK & YOUTUBE PAGES | @CIVILITY360

The State of Civility Youth Summit is developing Civility Solutions for our world through Civility In Action! Created to promote the pillars of civility through kindness, respect, love & action. Join Global World Civility Leader, Sir Clyde Rivers and Productive Business Civility Prof. Vernet Alin Joseph as we host civility in action. During the State of Civility Youth Summit, we Spoke to world leaders on the topic of "Dialogue About the Future & Voice of Global Youth."

A town hall meeting and platform to be modeled was presented by the founders of Civility360 Sir Clyde Rivers and Prof Vernet Alin Joseph. Our Civility 360 Town Hall Meeting brought leaders together for the purpose of civil dialogue on our current world issues. The theme from "Hostility to Civility" is needed now more than ever. We seek to have these types of town hall meetings in every city, state and country across the globe.

The founders of Civility360 Sir Clyde Rivers and Prof Vernet Alin Joseph present the State of Civility Summit Africa "The New African Narrative"

"FROM HOSTILITY TO CIVILITY"

A Cultural UNDERSTANDING OF RACE & RACISM

THURSDAY
JUNE 18TH, 2020
AT 6:00 PM PST | 9:00 PM EST

BUSINESS CIVILITY
PROF. VERNET A. JOSEPH
(AZ)

GLOBAL CIVILITY
SIR CLYDE RIVERS
(CA)

JACQUELINE EDWARDS
PRESIDENT OF THE ASSOCIATION OF BLACK ENFORCERS AND COMMUNITY LIASON FOR CORRECTIONS CANADA

DR. PHINEHAS KINUTHIA
CIVILITY DREAM ACTUALIZATION PERSON OF THE YEAR

DR. REBECCA HARPER
FAMILY CIVILITY

DR. LINDA LARA
2020 USA CIVILITY ICON, INNER-CITY CIVILITY

DR. SHARON ANDERSON ESQUIRE
AUTHOR OF EMOTIONAL CIVILITY

@CIVILITY360

JOIN US FOR THE CONVERSATION ON
CIVILITY360 FB AND YOUTUBE PAGES

A town hall meeting and platform to be modeled was presented by the founders of Civility360 Sir Clyde Rivers and Prof Vernet Alin Joseph. Our Civility 360 Town Hall Meeting brought leaders together for the purpose of civil dialogue on our current world issues. Discussing From Hostility To Civility "A Cultural Understanding of Race & Racism." Talking on the topics of Law Enforcement, Dream Actualization, Family Civility, Inner City Civility, and Emotional Civility.

The founders of Civility360 Sir Clyde Rivers and Prof Vernet Alin Joseph present the State of Civility Summit Caribbean "COVID ECONOMY 2020."

STATE OF CIVILITY SUMMIT

GLOBAL SPECIAL NEEDS INCLUSION FOR ALL

CHALLENGE CHAMPIONS & HEROES SUMMIT

BUSINESS CIVILITY
PROF. VERNET A. JOSEPH
(AZ)

WEDNESDAY | JULY 29TH
7 PM EST | 4 PM PST

GLOBAL CIVILITY
SIR CLYDE RIVERS
(CA)

DR. ROBIN LOCOCO   DR. RUBEN WEST   DR. REBECCA HARPER   DR. PENNY HEFLEBOWER   DR. TONY BRANCH   DR. GLENDON RUDDER

CHALLENGED CHAMPIONS & HEROES NATIONAL AWARENESS DAY.

@CIVILITY360   JOIN US FOR THE CONVERSATION ON CIVILITY360 FB AND YOUTUBE PAGES

The founders of Civility360 Sir Clyde Rivers and Prof Vernet Alin Joseph present the State of Civility Summit "Global Special Needs Inclusion For All." Challenged Champions and Heroes National Awareness Day

The founders of Civility360 Sir Clyde Rivers and Prof Vernet Alin Joseph present the Stay Alive Civility During "Suicide Prevention & Awareness Month." Featuring Amb. Psalm and Krystylle Richardson

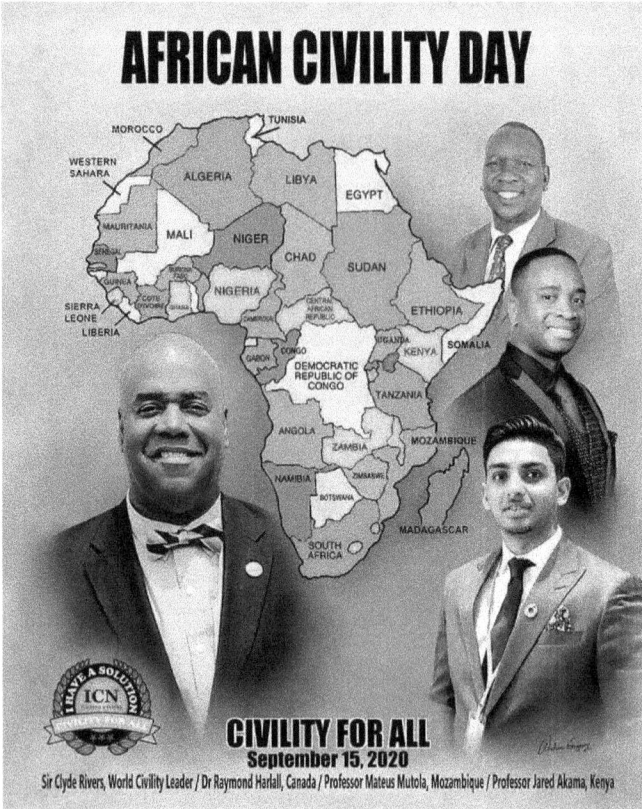

AFRICAN CIVILITY DAY

CIVILITY FOR ALL
September 15, 2020

Sir Clyde Rivers, World Civility Leader / Dr Raymond Harlall, Canada / Professor Mateus Mutola, Mozambique / Professor Jared Akama, Kenya

African Civility Day is a day were the continent of Africa shows kindness and respect to their fellow brothers and sisters across globe.

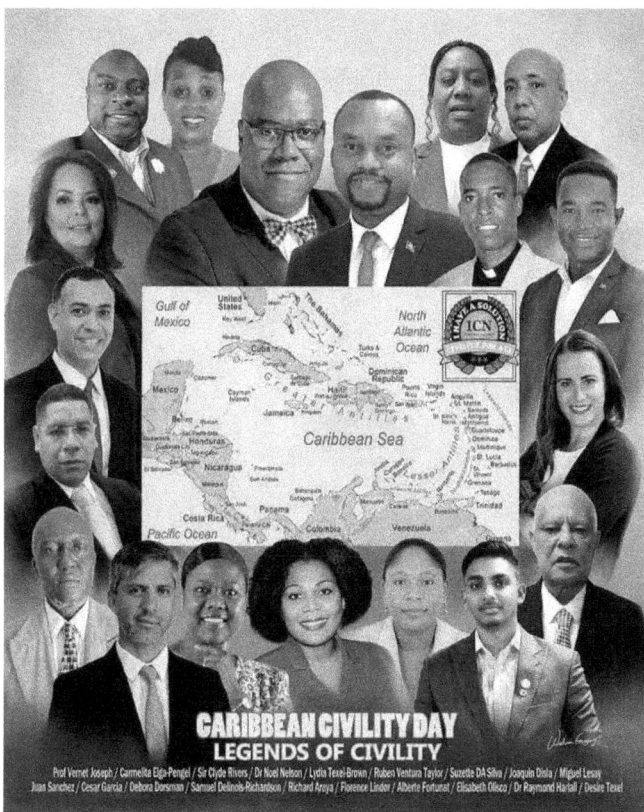

CARIBBEAN CIVILITY DAY
LEGENDS OF CIVILITY

Prof Vernet Joseph / Carmelita Elga-Pengel / Sir Clyde Rivers / Dr Noel Nelson / Lydia Texei-Brown / Ruben Ventura Taylor / Suzette DA Silva / Joaquin Disla / Miguel Lesay
Juan Sanchez / Cesar Garcia / Debora Dorsman / Samuel Delinois-Richardson / Richard Aroya / Florence Linder / Alberto Fortunat / Elisabeth Olisco / Dr Raymond Hartall / Desire Texel

Caribbean Civility Day is a day where the region of Caribbean shows kindness and respect to their fellow brothers and sisters across globe.

PASSING ON LEADERSHIP LEGACY

AFRICAN CLERGY CIVILITY

Sir Clyde Rivers ICN Founder / Dr Temesgen Fessanoye - Ginia Wolde Giorgis - Former President Ethiopia / Joyce Banda - Former President Malawi
Pierre Nkurunziza - President Burundi / Joaquim Chisano - Former President Mozambique / Dr Kenneth D. Kaunda - Former President Zambia

African Clergy Civility is where all the Clergy on the continent of Africa uniting to teach their congregations kindness and respect for all of humanity.

DR. CLYDE RIVERS - THE MAKING OF A WORLD CHANGER

Sir Clyde Rivers is a global world leader that uses his experience, expertise and influence to transform the hearts and minds of future world leaders.

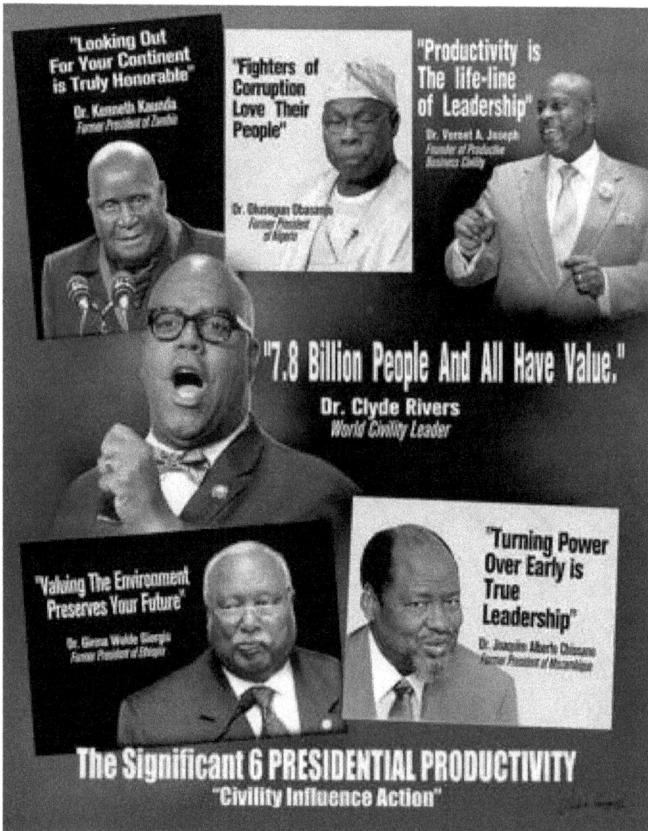

The Significant 6 PRESIDENTIAL PRODUCTIVITY
"Civility Influence Action"

Sir Clyde Rivers and Professor Vernet A. Joseph working with presidents to bring Productive Business Civility around the globe through civility in action.

98

SIR CLYDE RIVERS in a CLASS OF ROYALTY

Benedict Cumberbatch / Ringo Star / Sir Trevor McDonald / David Oyelowo/ Lord Eduardo Prodos / Rudolf Walker / Bill Gates / Bono / Patrick Stewart / Elton John / Naomi Harris

Sir Clyde Rivers, global world leader knighted into a class of royalty.

Civility at its finest!

CIVILITY FOR ALL

Sir Clyde Rivers is a global world leader that uses his experience, expertise and influence to transform the hearts and minds of future world leaders. I Have A Solution – Civility For All is a lifestyle not a movement.

WAGE CIVILITY 2021

SIR CLYDE RIVERS

PROFESSOR VERNET A. JOSEPH

BLESSED ARE THE PEACE MAKERS

Wage Civility this is our marching orders to bring kindness and respect to every individual and institution in the world.

ONE LAST MESSAGE

Congratulations on being the solution!

———⟨⟩———

We are proud of you for being a change agent and making the decision to better yourself, organization and institution by reading this book and making it a resource. I truly admire and respect you for taking the step to maximize your business, leadership and life.

Sir Clyde Rivers is the Global Civility Leader and Professor Vernet A. Joseph is the leading voice of Productive Business Civility globally, together they are recognized as the leading voices of Civility In Action.

As your organization is considering restructuring and operating in the new normal consider utilizing the Difference

Dialogue Training. If you are in need of Global Speakers and Trainers for your corporation, organization, institution or governmental structure, contact us at civility360@gmail.com and a member of the I Change Nations team will assist you.

As the world changes we will have to change with it. Having the right heart and mind is absolutely essential to making the transition seamless. Civility is the engine that makes the world go around. Tools like the book "When Histories Collide" on Diplomatic Diplomacy and "The Making of A World Changer" on seeing things from a world leaders view and "I Have A Solution" on race dialogue conversation are pivotal. We have worked in the Interfaith, NGO, United Nations, Presidential, and Kingdom levels. I Change Nations is the largest Culture of Honor on the planet and we are prepared to serve you.

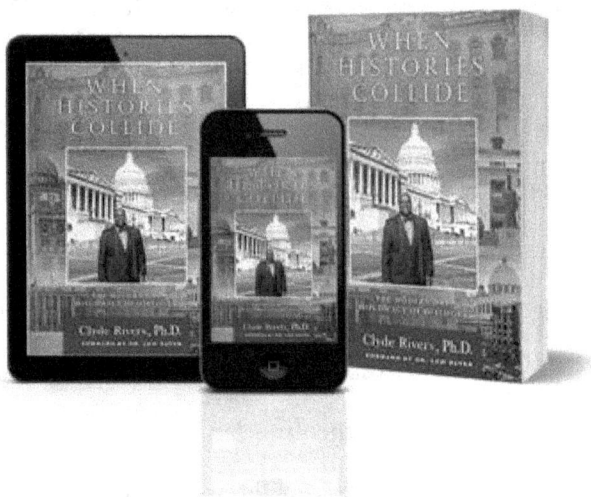

"When Histories Collide" on Diplomatic Diplomacy.

"The Making of A World Changer" on seeing things from a world leaders view.

"I Have A Solution" on race dialogue conversation.